Afternoons With Emily

Afternoons with Emily

Paul Quenon

Black Moss
Press
2011

Library and Archives Canada Cataloguing in Publication

Quenon, Paul
    Afternoons with Emily / Paul Quenon.

Poems.
ISBN 978-0-88753-492-8

    I. Title.

PS3567.U32A65 2011   811'.54   C2011-904619-9

Cover photo: Paul Quenon

Back cover author photo: Susan Seiller

Design: Kate Hargreaves

 Black Moss
EST.
1969 Press

Published by Black Moss Press at 2450 Byng Road, Windsor, Ontario, N8W 3E8 Canada. Black Moss books are distributed in Canada and the U.S. by LitDistCo. All orders should be directed to LitDistCo.

Black Moss Press books can also be found on our website www.blackmosspress.com

PRINTED IN CANADA

Contents

II Evenings with Rilke, translations

Aubades

Odes and Elegies

The Lives and Histories of Mad Monk

Oh, be just a bee—
sweet singer whose fearless hum
comes with a stinger.

Afternoons

Confessions of a Dead-Beat Monk

Of course, I've set the same bench
brushing off flies and thoughts,
how many years? What winters of
silence and summer variations,

what prodigy of mockingbirds
I've heard! And that kitchen job!
Broccoli and spuds on Mondays,
rice twice a week, and Oh,

toasted cheese sandwiches,
Fridays! This diet of psalms,
fifty and hundred, runs ever

on from bitter to sweet,

returns like the sun to bow
and stand. And I tread the same
stairs and stare at walls, blank
or lit rose and gold. I rise

with whippoorwills singing
at 3, though night ever keeps
its secret from me, 'til in
its treasure I'm locked.

Then will I be what always
has been, that enigma of
sameness between
now and then.

Paul Quenon

Hiker's Guide to the Monastery Knobs

In case you're lost:
Streams go down.
Follow that.

Upward trails go
towards the sun.
Follow that.

Old trail leads
to a lost colony
of Mayapples.

In parts unknown
inhabited by
redbud and dogwood—
trust these familiar friends.

Budding beeches
dismiss dry leaves to
wind in conversation with time,

puzzling over seasons
past and present
forgetting which is which.

Restless Silence

The enclosure wall runs the field,
ducks behind some pines
skirts the forest, dips and rises,
gently drops, then disappears.

Beyond, I can hear snow
melting in the woods.

What am I waiting for?
What enlightenment is in the sun
reflecting off the icy lake,
wearing it to a thin slick?

Dry grass in the wet field
is dusty with sunlight.
What is the grass waiting for?

A pigeon leaves a tree for another tree.

I can hear the sun
grazing the dusty grass,
until a breeze interrupts briefly
then settles for . . . a something . . .

Was it here already and gone?
Or was it only here
so I would come and wait?

Why this sadness when,
yielding to restlessness,
I rise and abandon what
never knows abandonment?

12   Paul Quenon

Marsh Hawk

The Marsh Hawk slow meanders
not far above the ground.
He tilts, and sways, and wanders
and cares not where he's found.

The thought he had he loses,
and wonders what he meant.
So casually he cruises
to follow where it went.

Along the lazy hills
he sees if all is still.
And if it isn't that,
beware you sorry rat!

Thunderclaps

A lumber truck hit
another bump in the road.

A shelf of snuff tins
collapsed in the attic.

A baseball rolled across
the corrugated roof.

A stack of marble slabs
toppled in the stoneyard.

A barrel rolled down
the basement stairs.

Grandma opens
a dresser drawer
in the next room.

Barn trusses crashed
beneath the hay load.

A load of granite
slid off the dump-truck.

Two boy giants
emptied boxes of marble balls
then poured lime chips
down the clothes chute.

Paul Quenon

A logging truck drove
across railroad ties
following the storm
off into the distance,
leaving us here
all washed clean.

Cooper's Hawk

Swift and straight, the Cooper's Hawk
flew far beyond this hill.
He'd never stop for idle talk,
my thoughts would make him ill.

The more he sees—he sees a lot—
the less he cares to stay.
What matters most, he's quickly caught,
not many get away.

A mind equipped with claws like that
can make me shrink and shy.
I hunker down and lay me flat—
he's sure to skin my hide.

Paul Quenon

Day Withholding

Some days the world holds off
at a distance, neither hot nor cold.
No promise is on the breeze,
birds converse elsewhere.

Heaven and earth—grey halves
of a closed shell, wherein I sit—
shriveled, loose nut, without
sap—some gnats, newly hatched

dance in my face, the only visitors
who like my smell and meager warmth.
Today, O let them have their way.

A Bench of Buzzards

A solemn court of buzzards,
atop a barren tree,
a black-robed bench of judges
paid little mind of me,

ignored my cautious glances—
impertinence they deemed
my tentative advances,
so negligible I seemed,

a man but of small moment.
My shaky step I checked—
they left with outspread mantles—
my bearing showed no depth.

One stayed behind and pondered:
"Were that poor twerp a bird,
and I a man out wandering
I'd deem him still absurd."

Paul Quenon

Three Stoics

Tiny ruined house
waist-high in thick, bare brambles
where buzzards keep watch:
where three scavengers,
feathers puffed against cold wind,
sit the roof—stirless.

Two Stoics, plus one,
ponder deeply rooms below
—their dim vacuity.
Sunk in their ruffs, they
ill regard any house warm, snug,
happy, full, silly.

Hermit's Yard

Sleek grackles slink
past black
one stretched neck
oil-slicked blue
checked out
this dude

dead set
one white-ringed
eye on him judged
him one dud

too wooden to slide
tip to tail
one slippery wave
sheer rhythm
high-step'n in grass
made smooth as wax
on jazz club floor

one up-beat leap
and off he flew
dropped behind
one white scat
to tell for me
that's enough of you

and for you O Hell
that's enough of that.

Paul Quenon

Log-Entry From Hermitage

What hulking dark hump-back shapes
appear on that sunny lawn?

Turkeys grazing at dignified pace,
each delicately balancing on two legs
as on waves, bearing Her Majesty's cargo,

and time to time, pausing to pick
at some particularity
no one else would see.

Occasionally, a mast is lifted
to see if all is well,
or one raised dark sails
to air out a bit, and welcome
breezes to her feathered arms.

They pass on into weeds, but one
stands awhile, tall—to tell me:
if you log an entry, Captain, Sir,
do write the entry well.

Task Assignments for Guardian Angels
commissioned by Fr. Matthew Kelty

For the Food Angel:

at my last meal on earth
no square fish without bones—a fish please,
with tail and head and an eye
that looks dead. No round flat salmon
or a frozen uniform-cut with bread crumbs for scales.

potatoes with a skin, not flakes, pearls or powder
watered and stirred, from a bag, box, can.

beets or carrots with tops, that grew under sunlight.

eggs cooked fresh out of a shell, not a wax carton,
or precooked, folded and frozen all in identical size.

lemonade from a lemon not powder,
no wine-cooler, but one
fermented to a finish.

For the Mortuary Angel:

Let me be buried in my own body, not:

half of me bled down a sewer

the rest filled with a chemical, to make me look
pink, un-dead, prepackaged and odorless.

Paul Quenon

Once I'm washed, clothed, lay me in church amid
murmur of psalms, not in a vault with hours
of chiller whine.

If needs be, use incense of sacred air, not talcum-and-soap smoke.

Be the burial Christian, where death is real,
not disguised, sanitized, Egyptian and pagan.

<u>For the Angel of Passage:</u>

Carry me away as a mango moon
in shaggy clouds to the west.

Reincarnation

Poets by thousands have sung
of cherry trees in bloom—
Thousands of bees are swarming
this humming, blooming tree.

Each a reincarnation seeks,
each a poem to taste, transport,
cap and seal in amber cell,
to emerge reborn a poet.

Paul Quenon

A Bend in the Season

Before autumn sets on,
time slows, birds grow still,
absent-minded and distant.

There's tinge of departure
in greens, before yellow whispers through.
Leaves, though humid, stiffen.

Sap, unseen, withdraws before
posture, breath, and muddled reason
bend you to a dryer season
that cordially bids: "Explore."

Hibernation

The wind had set
a cap of cold
upon my shaven skull

My brain got slow,
my thoughts withdrew
like rodents in the snow.

Paul Quenon

Evenings I

Glimpse

Deer, two deer flew 'cross my path.
A bound, a half, and vanished.
Glimpse, a fearful glimpse they snatched
at someone who is banished.

How I'd love their company!
But long is Eden gone.
Slain I'd be, one glance at God—
for death, sweet death I'd long.

Paul Quenon

On Passing Through An Intersection At Night

What's the prank!
To slam a pack
of cans against
the door?

"That was you,"
said a sweet
passenger in my
head to the self
assured at the wheel

who peered into the mirror
too late to fear
what's already done

a truck fender-ripped
under the stoplight.

"The only two cars here at night
said the cop, "and they bump into one another."

Dog-Star Sky

Under the Dog-
Star, one coyote
howled, stopped,
set off a pack
of yaps that tattered
night, its height
of glee gone
painful!

Misfits wailing
native claim,
frazzled me
spine to brain,
so alien I
underneath the
Dog-Star sky.

Paul Quenon

Roofless Sound

What is this sound thinning
to a veil, older than
walkways and walls,
longer remaining
than any trees?

What's this cricket sound
this canopy lifted to night
filling the garden where trees
under stars lean and listen
year after year?

A roofless sound they sustain,
inhabit awhile and perish,
and after a season
occupy once again.

What then is this sound?

Frozen Strife

A shimmering pool of
cricket chirrups
quickened the chill
heights. There Orion
stretched a bow
and let the flaming
Pleiades fly at Cygnus,
the Swan, far west.

Taurus with slow
head turned, gave
a bovine stare
perpetually waiting
to hear that doomed
bird drop.

Crickets sounded on
with little care
that Aries charged
with lowered horns
at the Lioness, spun
with up-lifted paw
and gaping jaw,
(mis-named Auriga.)

Misnamed all,
their frozen strife
by history long
forgot—quieted now
by a ceaseless, quivering
shimmering pool
of cricket chirrups.

Paul Quenon

Some
virgins

brought
lamps
with-
out
oil

Some,
oil
with
lamp.

With
nei-
ther
oil
nor
lamp

I'm
Bride

Cricket's Reverie

Summer now gone,
cricket's slow reverie
lingers on memory
of summer's song.

Less need be said
when things we said we'd do
were proved at last so few—
dreams left for dead.

Trees stand like harps,
strings bare just to the tops
where golden notes hang caught
as song departs.

Paul Quenon

Awakenings

Webs of clouds weave dreams
across the face of the moon
—sleeping, half smiling.

Muffled lowing of a cow
sends mother-comfort to
the hermit asleep
under the drifting moon.

. . .

"Strangeness! Strangeness!"
The owl cries
to the frosted world.

"That's a howling dog."
The monk awakened says.
"Strangeness! Strangeness!"
He goes back to sleep.

. . .

Nighttime troubadours
circle through woods and fields
—hounds singing hound love.

. . .

A mule cries out:
"I . . . I am the only mule!"

Afternoons with Emily

Then from a distance
another mule cried:
"I am the only mule . . . I!"
Night once more went mute.

• • •

Webs of clouds weave dreams
across the drifting moon—
sleeping, half smiling.

Paul Quenon

II Evenings With

Rilke

translations

Si l'on chante un dieu

If you sing of a god,
it responds with its silence.
None can approach a god
that is other than silent.

This invisible trade
making you to tremble,
is inheritance made
not for you but an angel.

Paul Quenon

The Panther

His gaze, from passing bars
has worn so blurred, it holds no more
than bars, a thousand bars.
Beyond the thousand—a world no more.

His limber pacing course
softly treads, in tightening circles spun.
It seems a dance of force
around which stands a great will—stunned.

At times, the eyes' shutters
will part—an image enters then
down stilled, tense limbs shudders,
where hoarded in the heart, it ends.

Moines Enormes . . .

Enormous, mighty monks all in their place
hold up eternity, heaven blooms
with iron and gold lineage, a tenacious race,
invincible, heated in a boom
of building monasteries, of menacing face.

Paul Quenon

Leaves are Falling

Leaves are falling, falling from a-far
like withering in heaven's distant garden,
falling with gestures of denial.

Through the night falls heavy earth
past all the stars in solitude.

All of us are falling, this hand falls,
the other one—look: it's in us all.

Yet One there is, with all this falling
always stays it softly in His Hand.

XXII Sonnets to Orpheus

We live—full drive!
Time walking slowly
takes all that lightly
in what abides

What hurries on
was already done.
What still carries on
hallows each one.

Boys, don't fling your life
into swiftness
and ventures of flight.

All is rested—look!
Darkness and brightness
blossom and book.

Paul Quenon

Year Circle . . .

Years circle in constant ways
for the tillers of land.
The Virgin and St. Ann
have each, in her turn, a say.

A word yet more ancient still
is added, it blesses,
and from earth there rises
verdure submissive in will,

which gives, through labor long
the grape of trust for us
and those who've passed beyond.

Quatrains Valasians #32

What god, what goddess
did surrender to space,
our sense to impress
with her lucid face?

His being, dissolved,
fills this pristine vale—
back-wash sways and stirs
with her vast nature.

He loves, she slumbers,
Fort Sesame's hold—
her body we enter
to sleep in his soul.

Paul Quenon

Vous Souvient-ils . . .

Do things you've lost remind
you the next day?
One last time they implore
—but there's no way—
to stay with you some more.

For the angel of lostness
brushed them with his heedless wing.
No more we hold them, keep them.

They received the stigmata
of absence, we knew not when.
Although windows were locked
a subtle wind came on them.

They'll step from that frame—
their precise procession of names.

What will their lives soon be?

—be no more human with us—
a life they loved. Will theirs be
long regrets in the sorry dust?

Or will it be that things will press
one another towards faster
forgetfulness? Will happiness
of vaguely being matter

Afternoons with Emily

take hold, returning them again
to the blind mother who touches
them, with scarcely any blame
for their having sustained
human thought?

Paul Quenon

Nous Nous Portons . . .

We carry on. But does weight
the dead add to earth stop her cold?
She moves on, despite such great
burden of the dead, untold.

Once inside her, they weigh not much—
the heavy dead; like a book that's read
she knows how it holds such—such
this heavy earth, who moves ahead.

Turnabout

The road from inwardness to greatness
goes through sacrifice — Kassner

Long he wrung it out watching.
Stars dropped to their knees
wrestled under his upward look.
Or kneeling, his outward gaze
and his incense did so insist
it made a god go weak
until it smiled at him from sleep.

Towers at his stare grew
tremulous: til he built them
up again in a moment's start!
How often the day-heavy
landscape rested in his
quiet thoughts at evening.

Beasts, grazing, trusted to range
his open gaze, and caged up lions
stared into freedom beyond grasp;
birds flying through felt it,
blossoms looked back at him
large as for children.

And a rumor—there was a Seer,
touched the humblest;
more tenuously clear,
stirred the women.
Seeing how long?

Paul Quenon

For how long profoundly needy,
pleading deep within looks?

When he, Attendant One, sat estranged; the Hotel's
distracted, disregarding room
dreary around him, and in the mirror avoided
again the room
and later from the torturous bed yet
again:
discussions in the air—

enigmatic comments
about his sensitive heart
over his thoroughly then aching flesh buried alive
heart still sensitive
is debated and judged
that this one had no love.

(And forbade him further communion.)

For looking, you see, has a limitation.
And the manifest world
wants to thrive in Love.
Work of the eyes is done,
now take up Heart-Work
upon the Images in you, caged within, which you
overpowered so: as of yet you know nothing of them.
See, inner Man, your inner Maiden,
this one wrung out
from a thousand Natures, this
wrested 'til now
but not yet loved Creature.

Afternoons with Emily

Abaudes

Hooded Sentinels

Venus stood bright above the court
in darkness awaiting
the tolling for Lauds, which
carried forth clear as
a cadet-angel's voice.

The cloister's darkened windows,
tall as hooded sentinels, stood
hollowed out by long
hallowed strokes of
eternity's bell, that
swayed to a stop so
time could resume and
Lauds another day begin.

Paul Quenon

Gone

Fog on the slope
lay like a notion
that obvious seemed
in a short spell
it shifted

and before you knew,
what you thought
you knew

was gone

Song of First Light

On the bench before dawn
a sparrow recites its one note,
as it did there

yesterday.

On the lawn-chair a robin
sings its song as it did there

yesterday,

Time, place and song,
—the same.

Summer is summer,
as it was last year,
and will be next.

Yet a bird, lost in a song of first light,
never knows repetition,
when all summers sing
as one timeless song
in each perfect call.

Paul Quenon

July First

With its single note, single note
a common sparrow cleanses space
for meditation.
Its insistence convinces
of many tones ranging within,
within its ring.

At the core of a distant tree
a new sun, red and warm, hides
itself—heart of a sacred world.

Robins—exhilarated—circle, close
and part in greeting
of another, another summer day.

The sun leans along, earth traveler,
'til veils and mirages of clouds
disclose it had lifted

at a distance,
a distance far,

far after all.

Narcissus Aged

Lighted surface ripples
caught his gaze, in nets
of cross-hatch waves that
moved and stayed.

Its shimmering veil
suspended thought 'til breezes dropped.

That water-curtain smoothed
to mirror distant clouds in
a lake of fathomless air.

He leaned down and caught a smile that
blossomed back—his face so small,
beneath such vastness—small.

Paul Quenon

Koi Pond

Koi fish, it's your hour!
Trees rimming the hills mimic
your blatant colour.

Clouds catching sunrise,
catch your orange, you brilliant Koi.
Oh! fly a fish kite.

Blizzards of buzzards
smoothly weave, lift and sally
'neath dappled red sky.

Wind-fall of elm leaves
sweep such sheer abundance by
of free-flung numbers.

Robins rove widely,
tight fists of intensity,
in fast free-form flock.

Koi fish, contented
in your crowded little pond,
our world's blowing wild!

Fading Meditation

I grasped at consciousness,
thought led me down,
my head went numb,
snatched to non-consciousness.

Thought sunk me, til half spent.
I went opaque,
then pulled awake,
confused, what thinking meant.

Strange, that old instruction:
"Follow your breath."
For God's sake, breath!
What's else left for this one!

Lost like a cork at sea,
there, where I am
is where I am,
all by necessity.

What's this? loss, or sheer bliss?
What's your notion
of the ocean?
What place could better this?

Paul Quenon

Ipsissime

Into
itself it
entered

reduced to
there and
then

solidified
to self-
sustained
self

diminished
  i
dotted
by itself

and was
itself the
dot.

Odes and Elegies

The Missing Pebble
For Fr. Louis Merton

On the pebble floor in the Chapter Room
one stone is missing.
Near the door, a char-hole remains
where a thunderbolt,
entered, struck, and removed
one rock only.

Forty years that hole remains,
the absent stone, un-replaced—
never seen again.

The very year that stone
was rendered electric,
a man, elected to be found
among monks he called "burnt men,"
was sundered electrically.

That precise wound
in the Chapter remains
a presence underfoot,
unnoted by monks
daily walking through.

Paul Quenon

In Praise of the Ballpoint Pens

What instrument of writing, I ask you,
is ever so fine to fiddle with?

When your mind goes blank,
too restless to think, down
on its plunger you set it—
click,
like a rocket launched it
and caught the feeble thing
—*thunk*,
on the bounce.

In distraction, unscrewed,
tightened, and loosened.
the plunger thumbed, in and out,
primed for a thought
that wouldn't come—not for a mind
idle so happily with a ballpoint pen!

When words finally flowed,
the roller point didn't, and left
but an etch on the page.

Tell me, is any Parker ink-pen
so heartedly flung?
—this easy ballpoint,
eager to get itself trashed!

Now, ink stains carpets,
pencil led poisons,

erasers chewed are
maddening to use,
—maddening too
not to chew.

Progress discarded
the quill's elegance,
the pencil's nostalgia,
the pen's expense and distinction;
has brought quantity, cheapness,
sleek advertisement props;
and computer's endless confusion,

but what, I tell you, is so
fiddle-worthy for your fickle mind,
what's thwarted your genius so
as your smeary old ballpoint pen?

Paul Quenon

Why He Got Divorced

"He has his issues:"
she said, and said no more.

Issues undisclosed:
one left, perhaps, in
a shirt pocket, one
carefully buttoned
on the hip—a volatile
issue or sensitive,
quick to emerge, then
dabbed with a tear.

There's his stubborn issue,
hard to place, or the fragile
one, finally addressed,
named, classified, hopelessly
reduced to shreds by some
much too pointed remarks—
marring an issue that sadly,
perhaps, waited to be taken up,
and when it was, another
popped up behind
with a soft rasp of its edges,
lifted to light of day,
pale and wan, itself
entailed with
another deeper issue
lying in the dark,
fold below fold of his
ever undisclosed issues.

I, Christopher

James asked Jesus to be seated on his left,
and John, seated on his right.
I never asked to be seated at all;
rather, He asked, to be seated on me.

Today I wade that precarious ford
between legend and the rock of fact,
bearing the immeasurable weight

of my own reward, to seat
the One who bears the weight
of this unbearable world.

Paul Quenon

Teresa and John

Nuns of Avila misunderstood
and reported that Teresa and John,
in conversation about things eternal,
had levitated above their chairs.

But their perception had gone askew.

For the two, steadied in Love Unmoveable,
had remained fixed, and the chairs, the room,
and the turning world had dropped aslant,
as they're wont to do.

Ancient Jade
for Jacqueline Chew

Surrounded by music
she stands stable as
an ancient jade.

In her eye no gleam
more than a dim
sanctuary lamp,

for she is elsewhere,
where music roams
in sacred rooms

of ancient nostalgia.

Paul Quenon

Elegy for Br. Alban,
30 Years with MS

No sound
other than acorns
dropping—
trees long fallen
heedless
in a muddy lake
he excavated once
in days of strength.

One small woodpecker
        tap—shy
tap. Shadow and light
fall on earth
no foot disturbed
but mine
and that but little.

Here I wait out
moments left draining
after the hull
of a patient man
has sunk
without a stir.

Trees swayed
in a fresh round
of breeze—
dropping acorns.

Feast of Archangels
for Fr. Matthew Kelty

Resting in a motor chair at window,
no longer tramping open fields to wade
where wind rolled waves of light and shadow,
his boredom aches at lawns cut flat and low.

Resting in a motor chair at window,
he asks Archangels, might there be a poem
strong enough to banish vicious mowers,
to justify each graceful blade that grows?

grand enough to open up broad visions
of grass returning tall from distant fields,
to stand in ranks and colorful divisions
on lawns from all banality now healed?

—where monsters of noise, exhaust, fumes, expense,
flee clover, Bluegrass, Cone Flowers, Queen Ann's Lace?

Paul Quenon

The Lives
and Histories
of Mad Monk

His Miraculous Conception

Sterile wives go to the Shrine
of St. John the Arab,
near Mar Gabriel,
to get water poured over them
from the holy monk's skull.
Then they are certain,
to bear a child.

A certain woman, childless,
badgered the poor old shrine-keeper
into pouring wine on her
instead.

And so was Mad Monk born,
his destiny set from the start.

Paul Quenon

Mad Monk

Christians of Byzantium, about to eat,
blessed a leaf of lettuce
for fear a demon
perched there.

Mad Monk bit off the demon,
spit him out and
threw away the lettuce.

Mad Monk, bored

with the world,
bored with himself,
stopped everything
—just stopped—
until Boredom,
never stopped by anything
but nothing,
went away
bored.

Paul Quenon

Mad Monk's Rosary

Mad Monk handed his rosary
to a curious Jew who'd heard
rosaries sometimes turned gold.

The man took the tarnished thing,
looked,
handed it back. It had
turned gold in his hand.

"Pretty slick!" he said,
and walked away.

Mad Monk stood still
baffled.

Mad Monk's Boyhood

When a boy, Mad Monk
sat in front of the television
with a spoon. The Psychic
on the screen said: When
I count 3, everyone's spoon
will bend. With the slightest
effort it bent.

His mother was put out:
"Who ruined that spoon?"

So he pulled easy,
straightened it out,
and never tried that
trick again.

Paul Quenon

Cow Patch

Set down by a cow patch
to meditate, Mad Monk
ended up bellowing
back at the cows.

On Winter Evenings

he served the donkeys
warm water before bedtime,

closed the cozy barn
and went out and slept
in the starlight,
never made them
work a day in their lives—

"Lap donkeys," he called them.

Paul Quenon

Mad Monk To a Neighbour Who Lost His Dog

"No, your dog is not lost, sir.

She is losing you and is out
cheerfully following her nose
where she can be just a dog awhile,
without any interference by
being your pet.

Home is for two-footers
and she can very well find you there
from anywhere from 20 miles around.

If she's worth anything at all,
she'll remember you're
at home—lost,
in Hell
and will soon
come loping back to you."

Neighbour's Question:

"Isn't it unhealthy
living with chickens and
goats in your hermitage?"

Said he: "They haven't got sick yet."

Paul Quenon

His Levitation

"What are you doing
up there?" said the Abbot
who found him floating in prayer.
"I've stayed where I was.
You and the turning earth
have gone lopsided."

No Plans

A certain hermit sent a message
from his deathbed
to Mad Monk:

"I will soon die. Come. We must bid farewell."

Mad Monk sent his reply to the hermit:

"Should I busy myself
with someone still so full of plans?"

Paul Quenon

Dutch Door

Mad Monk had two doors—
or one, with a swinging panel
below, kept unlocked
for foxes, coons and rabbits
to come and go.

"Don't worry, he'll leave soon. . ."

The upper half had a lock
against human intruders.

Brief Palace

To accommodate him in old age,
brother monks built him a new hermitage,
complete with electricity, tap water,
shower and boiler.
He called it a palace and
gratefully moved in.

But soon after his empty old shack,
where he lived 30 years
was plowed to a heap.
On that day, Mad Monk was found
slumped over in his new armchair,

no longer of this world.

Paul Quenon

Reincarnation

Mad Monk needed more meditation.
He died and happily came back
as a quiet cow on a grassy hillside.

But at times she forgot herself
and biblically bellowed out at
the heedless world:

hhuuuunnnwaaawwh

The world, even then,
remained unconverted.

Afterword, My Last Poem

When I write my last poem
it will not say goodbye
to poetry, but hello to itself,

will heave a glad sigh
it got into the world
before the door closed,

will look to its companion poems,
that it might have place
among these orphans,

that they might reach out hands
in company to go together
into oblivion or into memory,

or to some secret cove
where eternity sits,
from time to time, and reads.

Paul Quenon

Paul Quenon, OSCO, has been a Trappist monk for 50 years. He lives and works at the Abbey of Gethsemani where he cooks, sings in the choir, hikes, meditates outdoors, and somewhere in between puts words together into poems, and turns his gaze into the camera lens to photograph what he loves. He is the author of *Terrors of Paradise, Laughter: My Purgatory,* and *Monkswear.*